LEXINGTON PUBLIC LIBRARY

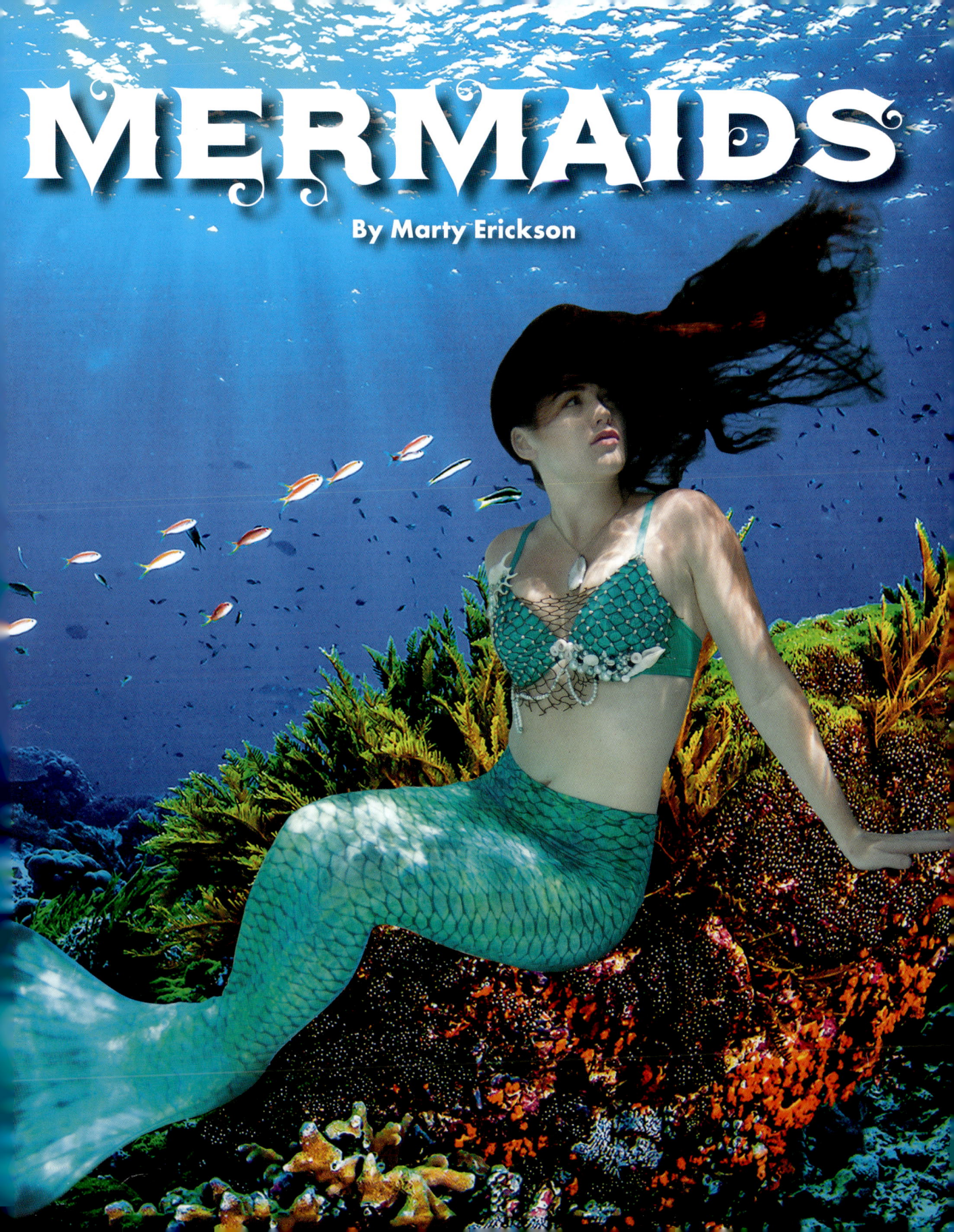

MERMAIDS

By Marty Erickson

Published by The Child's World®
1980 Lookout Drive • Mankato, MN 56003-1705
800-599-READ • www.childsworld.com

Photographs ©: Peter Leahy/Shutterstock Images, cover (mermaid), 1 (mermaid); Irina Markova/Shutterstock Images, cover (background), 1–3 (background); Shutterstock Images, 5, 6–7, 11, 13, 14, 15, 19, 20, 24; Yasuyoshi Chiba/AFP/Getty Images, 9; Maksym Veber/Shutterstock Images, 16; Andrea Izzotti/Shutterstock Images, 17, 23; Ari Wid/Shutterstock Images, 21

Copyright © 2022 by The Child's World®
All rights reserved. No part of this book may be reproduced or utilized in any form or by any means without written permission from the publisher.

ISBN 9781503849754 (Reinforced Library Binding)
ISBN 9781503850804 (Portable Document Format)
ISBN 9781503851566 (Online Multi-user eBook)
LCCN 2021939491

Printed in the United States of America

Table of CONTENTS

CHAPTER ONE
Something in the Water...4

CHAPTER TWO
History of Mermaids...8

CHAPTER THREE
Scales and Fish Tails...12

CHAPTER FOUR
Mermaids Today...18

Glossary...22

To Learn More...23

Index...24

CHAPTER ONE

SOMETHING IN THE WATER

Kaylee and her dad were out **kayaking**. They lived on the Isle of Man near Ireland. There were many beautiful sea caves along the shore. Kaylee dreamed of seeing a mermaid one day. There were many legends around the island about mermaids.

The pair continued to paddle. As they rounded the entrance to a rocky cave, they heard a splash. But they did not see anything. Whatever had been there disappeared. A haunting whistle echoed against the rock walls.

People can kayak on the sea and other bodies of water.

Mermaids are mythical sea creatures that are half human and half fish.

Kaylee's dad said something about a fish. He said the wind made the whistling sound. But the girl was sure it was a mermaid. She hoped she was one step closer to seeing one in real life.

Mermaids are **mythical** creatures. Legends about mermaids are ancient. But no matter how old the legends are, mermaids continue to capture people's imaginations.

CHAPTER TWO

HISTORY OF MERMAIDS

Stories about mermaids go back thousands of years. Some stories say mermaids have magical powers. Mermaids can be helpful or harmful to people.

One legend from the Middle East said a merman taught people how to read. Merfolk were respected. But not all legends described mermaids as kind or helpful. In Europe, **folklore** about mermaids was different.

Mermen called Tritons are part of Greek mythology.

Instead of being helpful and wise, European stories said mermaids were dangerous. If a sailor saw a mermaid, that was a sign the ship was going to crash. As with other legends about mermaids, European stories said mermaids had magical powers. But mermaids did not always use their powers for good.

Many legends say merfolk love music. Mermaids often have beautiful singing voices. People can hear the singing from far away. In some stories, mermaids **lure** sailors away with their songs. They pull sailors over the edge of their ships. Sometimes the sailors jump into the sea. These singing mermaids are sometimes called sirens.

In some stories, mermaids lure men underwater to their deaths.

CHAPTER THREE
SCALES AND FISH TAILS

Many legends about merfolk describe them similarly. In most stories, mermaids and mermen have the head and upper body of a human. They have the lower body of a fish. Merfolk have tails and **scales**. Illustrations of mermaids often show their tails as being brightly colored.

Stories about mermaids often describe them as **social**. They live with other merfolk in an underwater community. But not all mermaid legends agree on everything.

Most mermaids look like regular humans from the waist up. Their tails can be many different colors.

human upper body

scales

tail

fin

In some stories, merfolk can go back and forth between the water and the land.

One detail that is different from story to story is whether a mermaid's appearance is permanent. Some stories say a mermaid stays in the water her whole life. However, other myths say merfolk can take their tails on and off. In some stories, mermaids marry human men. They leave the water for land.

One mythical mermaid-like creature is a selkie. Selkies are similar to mermaids, except they take the form of a seal. They can take their seal skins on and off. A selkie buries her seal skin to hide it. If a person steals a selkie's skin, the selkie is forced to stay with the person.

Selkie stories are common in northern Scotland. The word selkie *means* seal *in Celtic languages.*

Mermaids look more human in some stories than in others.

Legends also differ on how mermaids breathe. Some say they can breathe both underwater and above water. Gills are how they breathe underwater. Lungs allow mermaids to breathe air. But other myths say they either only breathe air or only breathe underwater. For those mermaids, it is not possible to do both. If a mermaid could only breathe air, she would need to stay close to the surface in order to breathe often.

In some stories, mermaids can only breathe underwater.

CHAPTER FOUR
MERMAIDS TODAY

Legends of mermaids are ancient. But researchers believe real animals may have inspired the myths. One such animal may be the manatee. A manatee is a marine **mammal**. Manatees come to the surface of the water to breathe.

Hundreds of years ago, people did not know about manatees. For example, Christopher Columbus was a famous sailor from Italy. He spotted a manatee near Florida in 1493. But he did not know what a manatee was. He believed he saw a mermaid.

Early explorers may have mistaken manatees and other similar animals for mermaids.

Mermaids still capture people's imaginations. New stories about mermaids continue to come out. Many movies include mermaids. For example, Disney's *The Little Mermaid* is about a mermaid named Ariel. The movie is based on the folktale by Hans Christian Andersen.

This statue of the Little Mermaid is in Copenhagen, Denmark.

People can perform as merfolk in aquariums, theaters, and more.

Additionally, some people work as mermaids. They use fake tails. They swim in aquariums or the ocean. Working mermaids train a long time to hold their breath underwater. Sometimes they use air hoses to breathe.

Mermaids are not real. But they continue to inspire people. From magic to manatees, mermaids live in people's imaginations. Some people pretend to be mermaids. People will continue to make new stories about mermaids.

GLOSSARY

folklore (FOHK-lor) Folklore is the stories and beliefs that a group of people have passed down through the generations. Mermaids in European folklore are described differently than in stories from the Middle East.

kayaking (KY-ack-eeng) Kayaking is paddling a long, narrow boat called a kayak. Kayaking can be done on lakes, rivers, and the sea.

lure (LOOR) To lure is to draw close. In some stories, mermaids lure sailors into the ocean with their singing.

mammal (MAM-uhl) A mammal is an animal that gives birth to live young that drink milk. Manatees are a type of marine mammal.

mythical (MITH-ih-kuhl) When something is mythical, there are many legends about it. Mermaids are mythical creatures.

scales (SKAYLZ) Scales are smooth, overlapping plates that grow from a fish's skin. A mermaid's tail is covered in colorful scales.

social (SOH-shuhl) To be social means to want to spend time with other creatures of the same type. Some stories say mermaids are social.

TO LEARN MORE

In the Library

Alberti, Theresa Jarosz, and John Willis. *Mermaids*. New York, NY: AV2 by Weigl, 2020.

Drimmer, Stephanie Warren. *Beneath the Waves*. Washington, DC: National Geographic Kids, 2021.

O'Brien, Cynthia. *Mermaid Myths*. New York, NY: Gareth Stevens Publishing, 2018.

On the Web

Visit our website for links about mermaids:

childsworld.com/links

Note to Parents, Teachers, and Librarians: We routinely verify our Web links to make sure they are safe and active sites. So encourage your readers to check them out!

INDEX

appearance, 12–14

breathing, 17, 18, 21

Columbus, Christopher, 18

Europe, 8–10

Little Mermaid, The, 20

manatees, 18, 21
Middle East, 8
music, 10

sailors, 10, 18
selkies, 15
sirens, 10

tails, 12–14, 21

ABOUT THE AUTHOR

Marty Erickson is a writer living in Minnesota. They write books for young people full time and like to go hiking.